WORLD WAR II

THE US HOME FRONT DURING WORLD WAR II

by Ryan Gale

FOCUS READERS®
VOYAGER

www.focusreaders.com

Focus Readers is distributed by North Star Editions:
sales@northstareditions.com | 888-417-0195

Produced for Focus Readers by Red Line Editorial.

Content Consultant: Dr. Gideon Mailer, Associate Professor of History, University of Minnesota Duluth

Photographs ©: AP Images, cover, 1, 35; Shutterstock Images, 4–5, 7, 9, 10–11, 13, 14–15, 21, 31, 39, 40–41; Marjory Collins/Library of Congress, 17; Edward Meyer/Library of Congress, 18; Ansel Adams/Library of Congress, 22–23; Clem Albers/Library of Congress, 25; Red Line Editorial, 27; Gordon Parks/Library of Congress, 28–29; FPG/Archive Photos/Getty Images, 33; Bettmann/Getty Images, 36–37; Library of Congress, 43; Howard Liberman/Library of Congress, 45

Library of Congress Cataloging-in-Publication Data
Names: Gale, Ryan, author.
Title: The US home front during World War II / Ryan Gale.
Description: Lake Elmo, MN : Focus Readers, [2023] | Series: World War II | Includes index. | Audience: Grades 4-6
Identifiers: LCCN 2022005185 (print) | LCCN 2022005186 (ebook) | ISBN 9781637392836 (hardcover) | ISBN 9781637393352 (paperback) | ISBN 9781637394335 (pdf) | ISBN 9781637393871 (ebook)
Subjects: LCSH: World War, 1939-1945--United States--Juvenile literature.
Classification: LCC D769 .G35 2023 (print) | LCC D769 (ebook) | DDC 940.53/73--dc23/eng/20220210
LC record available at https://lccn.loc.gov/2022005185
LC ebook record available at https://lccn.loc.gov/2022005186

Printed in the United States of America
Mankato, MN
082022

ABOUT THE AUTHOR

Ryan Gale is an artist and writer from Minnesota. He loves reading and writing about history.

TABLE OF CONTENTS

CHAPTER 1

WORLD WAR II HITS HOME

On September 1, 1939, Germany launched a massive invasion. More than one million soldiers marched into Poland. Bombers flew overhead, and thousands of tanks plowed across the country's border. They seized control and refused to leave. So, two days later, Poland's **allies** Britain and France declared war on Germany. World War II (1939–1945) had begun in Europe.

In September 1939, German soldiers attacked Warsaw, Poland's capital city.

However, the United States stayed neutral. Most people in the United States didn't want their country to go to war. President Franklin Delano Roosevelt knew this. But he wanted to be ready in case the country was attacked. So, he began preparing for war. He had factories in the United States start making airplanes, tanks, guns, and bombs. This increase in production created new jobs. It helped the US economy grow.

In 1941, the United States began selling weapons to countries fighting against Germany. It also limited trade with Japan, Germany's ally. But US forces stayed out of the fighting. Then, on December 7, 1941, Japan bombed a US naval base at Pearl Harbor in Hawaii. The United States declared war on Japan shortly afterward.

After the attack on Pearl Harbor, many Americans were eager to support the war effort.

Japan's attack badly damaged 18 of the 70 US ships anchored at Pearl Harbor.

Millions of people joined the military. Many were sent overseas to fight. But some were stationed on the home front. They prepared to protect the country from enemy attacks.

The US government also took action. US troops needed weapons and supplies. To meet this demand, the US government paid to build more equipment and factories. Before the war, most manufacturing took place in northern states.

The South had mainly focused on agriculture. During the war, however, the government built new manufacturing plants in the South. Some produced ships and airplanes. Others made materials such as rubber or steel. Together, they created thousands of jobs. As a result, the South had a huge boom in production. Some companies and workers even moved from the North.

Some industries, such as iron, stayed mainly in northern states. But companies often shipped materials to the South for production.

Meanwhile, researchers were studying ways to create new weapons and technology. They made many advancements during the war. Some helped improve **radar** and computers. Others created the first nuclear weapons.

The US government began the Manhattan Project in 1942. Hundreds of scientists from

So many people worked on the Manhattan Project that towns were built for them to live in.

across the country worked together. They created two atomic bombs. US planes dropped these bombs on two Japanese cities, Hiroshima and Nagasaki, in August 1945. The bombs played a role in ending the war. However, they also caused massive amounts of death and destruction.

Japan surrendered less than a month later. World War II had ended. But the world would never be the same. Major changes had taken place both on the US home front and abroad.

We Can Do It!
POST FEB. 15 TO FEB. 28
WAR PRODUCTION CO-ORDINATING COMMITTE

CHAPTER 2

WOMEN AND THE WAR EFFORT

During World War II, **civilians** on the US home front supported the war effort in many ways. Women played a crucial role in this work. To fight the war, the US military needed thousands of vehicles and weapons. Factories across the country worked around the clock to make them. Meanwhile, farms had to provide food for thousands of soldiers. These farms and factories needed many workers. But millions of men had

Posters featuring Rosie the Riveter encouraged women to join the war effort.

left their jobs to join the military. Women stepped in to fill these positions.

Before the war, women were often expected to have only certain jobs, such as nurses or teachers. During the war, however, women took on many new types of work. They operated machinery, welded, and farmed.

Some women joined groups such as the Red Cross and the American Women's Voluntary Services. These groups raised money for the war. They collected food and supplies to send to soldiers. Volunteers also drove ambulances or worked in hospitals.

In addition, nearly 350,000 women joined the military during World War II. Women weren't allowed to have combat roles. So, some worked in labs or offices. Others drove or fixed vehicles. Female pilots helped test and fly planes.

Welders joined together parts to help build ships and airplanes.

Women did military research as well. For example, several hundred women worked on the Manhattan Project. Women also worked as code breakers. They decoded enemy messages.

After the war, many women wanted to keep their jobs. But they were often replaced by men who had returned from fighting.

CHAPTER 3

DOING WITHOUT

World War II affected what people could make and buy. Before the war, most US factories had made commercial goods, such as cars and appliances. Now, they needed to make weapons and other supplies for the military.

To help make this change, President Roosevelt created the War Production Board. This group was in charge of what factories produced. It also managed the raw materials that factories needed.

Some US car factories began making tanks to help the war effort.

These materials included steel, rubber, and oil. Because factories were making so many supplies, demand for raw materials was much higher than usual. It was often hard to get enough of them.

To help solve this problem, the government asked people to collect scraps for recycling. Communities across the country gathered leftover metal and rubber items. People collected tin cans, tires, and machines with metal parts. The government recycled these items. It used them to build ships, airplanes, and tanks.

People also collected food scraps, such as fat and bones. Fat was used to make explosives. Bones were used to make glue and fertilizer.

The war affected other resources, too. For example, military vehicles needed huge amounts of gasoline. And soldiers needed food. To make sure these resources didn't run out, the

People collected and recycled old metal items to help with shortages of steel, tin, and aluminum.

government limited how much civilians could buy. This process was called rationing, and it applied to many goods. Gasoline was rationed. So were coal and tires. Certain foods were rationed as well. They included butter, sugar, coffee, and meat.

If people wanted to buy rationed goods, they needed ration stamps. The government gave a set amount of these stamps to each adult and child in the country. By giving these stamps to a store,

Children often helped grow victory gardens for their families or communities.

people could buy a certain amount of a rationed item. If their stamps ran out, people couldn't buy any more. They had to wait until they got more stamps from the government.

The government also encouraged people to grow their own food. Some people planted gardens in their yards. Others made gardens in parks or other public spaces. These areas were known as "victory gardens." Some people canned the food they grew. That helped it last longer.

Going to war was very expensive. To help pay for it, the government raised taxes. It also encouraged Americans to buy war bonds. A bond is similar to a loan. When people purchase bonds, the government pays them back a slightly higher amount after a set time. The US government raised billions of dollars this way. It used the money to pay war costs.

Wartime limits were difficult for many people. People had to go without many items. They struggled with food shortages and high taxes. However, many Americans saw enduring these problems as their **patriotic** duty. They made sacrifices to help their country win the war.

CONSIDER THIS

Would you endure hardship in order to help your country? Why or why not?

THE BLACK MARKET

Not all Americans followed the rationing rules. Some people turned to the black market. They bought and sold rationed goods illegally. For example, some merchants sold rationed goods to people without stamps if they paid higher prices. Merchants might also sell more goods than the limit. Gasoline and meat were the most common black-market goods.

Merchants were supposed to bring used stamps to collection centers. There, the stamps would be destroyed. But some merchants kept used stamps instead of returning them. They sold these stamps on the black market so people could use them again. People could also buy fake or stolen stamps.

People who were caught buying or selling goods on the black market faced fines and jail time. However, the government had few resources

People who bought or sold rationed goods without the correct stamps could be fined as much as $10,000.

to fight the problem. Only a small number of cases went to court.

In April 1945, reporter Ray Sprigle went undercover. He wanted to expose the illegal sale of rationed meat. Sprigle traveled across Pennsylvania. In three weeks, he managed to buy more than 2,000 pounds (907 kg) of meat. He also bought 10,000 meat ration stamps. Sprigle published articles about his experience. His articles convinced the government to take greater steps to stop the black market.

CHAPTER 4

PRISONERS AT HOME

While soldiers were fighting battles in Europe and Asia, Americans faced problems at home. **Racism** was one of them. After the bombing of Pearl Harbor, military leaders were afraid Japan would attack the West Coast. They also feared that Japanese Americans would side with Japan. Approximately 120,000 people of Japanese ancestry lived in the United States in

During World War II, more than 30,000 Japanese Americans served in the US military.

1941. Most of them were US citizens. And most lived in California, Oregon, and Washington.

On February 19, 1942, President Roosevelt issued Order 9066. This order allowed the US military to force people to move if they were considered a security threat. Military leaders quickly targeted Japanese Americans in West Coast states. The US military told them to move inland. Approximately 8,000 people did. However, most did not. So, in March 1942, soldiers began moving people by force. Many families had only a few days to prepare. They had to sell or leave behind everything they couldn't carry with them.

Japanese Americans were sent to assembly centers in the western United States. They were detained at these centers while the military built more permanent places. During the summer and fall of 1942, Japanese Americans were

At some assembly centers, people had to live in buildings that used to be horse stalls.

sent to these new camps. The military called them “relocation centers.” But they were more like prisons. People lived crowded together in small rooms. The camps were surrounded by barbed-wire fences and guard towers. People were not allowed to leave without permission.

Many Japanese Americans resisted relocation. Some went into hiding. Others protested. They called out the US government for violating their rights. Japanese Americans hadn’t been charged with any crimes. Yet they were held in jail-like camps. They were also forced to answer loyalty questions. One question made them promise to serve in the US military. Another had them swear not to serve Japan's emperor. No other Americans were asked loyalty questions.

In response to this unfairness, some Japanese Americans led protests in the camps. People who resisted were often sent to jail or punishment camps. Conditions there could be even worse.

By the end of 1944, the United States had won many battles against Japan in the South Pacific. Military leaders no longer considered Japan a threat to the West Coast. So, they began releasing people from the camps in January 1945.

Many Japanese Americans returned home to find their property damaged or stolen. Many lost farms or businesses. They also faced

discrimination. Some businesses wouldn't hire or sell to Japanese Americans.

After the war, the US government gave money to former detainees for lost or damaged property. However, the payments were much less than what people had lost. And they didn't make up for the way people's rights had been violated.

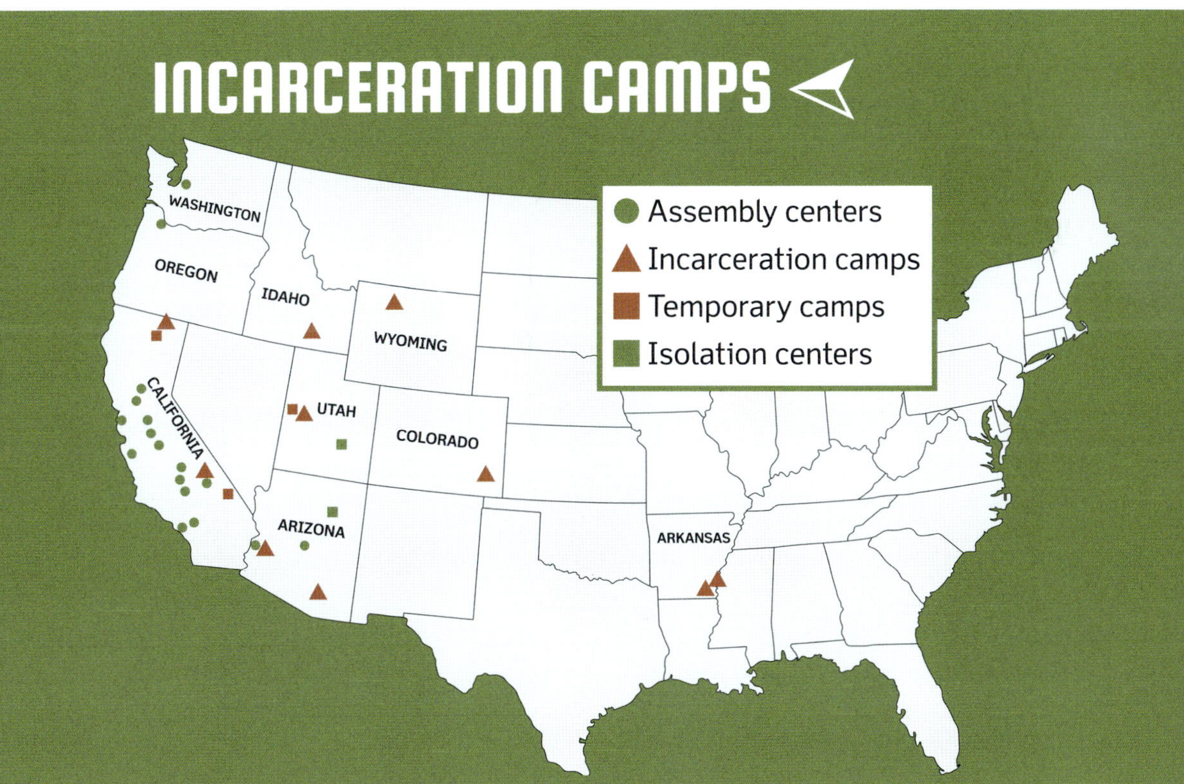

CHAPTER 5

DOUBLE VICTORY

Black Americans also faced discrimination during World War II. As wartime production boomed, thousands of jobs opened in the defense industry. But few Black Americans could get these jobs. Employers often hired white workers instead.

In June 1941, A. Philip Randolph planned a huge march on Washington, DC. Randolph was a Black **civil rights** leader. He wanted to protest the problems Black workers faced.

A. Philip Randolph was an activist. He called for better jobs and better pay for Black workers.

President Roosevelt wanted to stop the march. He thought it would lead to rioting. However, Randolph would not cancel the march unless Roosevelt took action to stop discrimination. So, on June 25, Roosevelt signed Order 8802. This order banned discrimination in the defense industry. Randolph called off the march on Washington shortly after.

Order 8802 was a major victory for civil rights. It also led to a mass migration. In the early 1940s, most Black Americans lived in southern states. Many lived in poverty. Jobs in the defense industry paid well. But in the South, these jobs were hard for Black workers to get. So, thousands of Black Americans moved to other regions. They found jobs at factories in the North and West.

Many Black workers still faced discrimination. Some employers refused to hire Black Americans

Between 1940 and 1945, US factories built more than 300,000 airplanes.

despite Order 8802. Those who did hire Black Americans often refused to hire Black women. Black workers were often paid lower wages. And few were promoted to leadership jobs. Some companies let them work only night shifts. If Black workers spoke up, they were often fired.

Segregation, which is the separation of people based on race, also continued. Black and white employees usually worked in separate groups. They had separate bathrooms and drinking fountains. Clashes between Black and white workers sometimes led to violence and rioting.

Government officials did little to help Black workers. They chose to focus on winning the war and not on civil rights. However, activists did not give up. For instance, Randolph organized marches to end segregation. And Mary McLeod Bethune asked the government to expand the role of Black women in the military.

The press also got involved. In 1942, the *Pittsburgh Courier* began a civil rights campaign. In addition to defeating the nation's enemies overseas, it urged people to fight the enemies of civil rights at home. The campaign was called the

CONSIDER THIS

How do newspapers and other media shape what people think and care about?

In the 1900s, the *Pittsburgh Courier* was one of the largest Black-owned newspapers in the United States.

Double Victory, or Double V, campaign. It called for equal opportunities in the military and defense industry. Additional goals included voting rights and equal pay.

Double V clubs sprang up around the country. Members held protests. They also met with leaders in business and politics. Civil rights activists didn't achieve most of their goals during World War II. But their work set the stage for the civil rights movement of the 1950s and 1960s.

THE DETROIT RACE RIOT

More than one million Black Americans migrated during World War II. Many left southern states and moved to northern cities.

In Detroit, Michigan, the arrival of so many people created a housing shortage. Detroit was segregated. Black residents could live only in certain areas. These areas became overcrowded. Many Black families had to live in cramped apartments. Some tried to move to white neighborhoods. But white residents blocked them.

Detroit's Black residents also faced racism at work and in public. Fights sometimes broke out. On June 20, 1943, Black and white residents began fighting at a crowded park. The crowd turned into an angry mob. Groups of Black and white rioters roamed the city's streets. Some

In June 1943, racial tensions in Detroit, Michigan, erupted into a deadly riot.

looted stores and flipped cars. White police officers targeted Black rioters. They shot and killed several Black men.

The riot lasted for three days. It ended only after soldiers with armored vehicles arrived. Thirty-four people were killed during the riot. Several hundred were arrested. It was one of the largest race riots in US history.

News of the riot spread across the world. Some Americans thought the riot was planned by German or Japanese spies. Others blamed Black residents of Detroit. Nothing was done to solve the racial issues that were the real cause.

SAMPLES
305
UNCENSORED LETTER

CHAPTER 6

THE WAR ON WORDS

During a war, information can be as important as weapons. Shortly after declaring war on Japan, Congress passed the War Powers Act. Part of this law involved controlling the information going into and out of the country.

In times of war, **censorship** can keep important information from reaching enemies. It can also stop discouraging news from being made public. Limiting bad news is meant to improve **morale**.

Workers at a censor station in New York check international mail for restricted material.

President Roosevelt created the Office of Censorship on December 19, 1941. This group set up censoring stations all over the United States.

Some stations opened mail from overseas. Censor agents checked the mail and deleted restricted material. This material was information that might help the enemy, such as the locations of factories or military bases. Censor agents often covered restricted material with black ink. Or they cut it out with scissors. Agents might destroy items that contained large amounts of restricted material.

Some censoring stations monitored international telephone calls. Other stations were placed at US borders. These stations checked documents being carried by people leaving the country. Newspapers and radio stations had to deal with censorship, too. The Office of

Censorship made guidelines listing what they could and could not say.

Censorship was unpopular in the United States. Some people tried to get around it. They wrote using secret codes and invisible ink. Or they hid letters inside other packages. Punishment for trying to evade censorship included fines and imprisonment. Censoring finally ended in August 1945, shortly after Japan surrendered.

TYPES OF RESTRICTED MATERIAL

WAR PLANS OR NEGOTIATIONS

INFORMATION ABOUT ENEMY ATTACKS

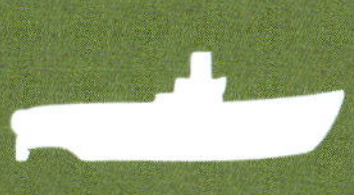

MOVEMENTS OF ARMED FORCES, SHIPS, OR PLANES

LOCATIONS OF FACTORIES OR DEFENSES

FACTS ABOUT WEAPONS OR PRISONERS OF WAR

TRAVEL PLANS OF THE US PRESIDENT

BUY WAR BOND

CHAPTER 7

PROPAGANDA

In addition to stopping some information from spreading, the US government also sent out information. President Roosevelt created the Office of War Information (OWI) in June 1942. This group was in charge of propaganda. Propaganda is information that is meant to affect people's beliefs and behaviors.

The OWI produced many types of propaganda. Some urged Americans to take certain actions,

A propaganda poster encourages Americans to support their country by purchasing war bonds.

such as joining the military. Other propaganda stirred people's emotions. It might inspire national pride. Or it might create fear and anger toward enemy armies. It reminded Americans why their country was at war, and it motivated them to keep fighting.

Posters were cheap and easy to display. So, they were a common form of propaganda. The OWI created many types of posters. Some showed soldiers doing heroic deeds. Some had inspiring images of farmers or factory workers. Others had disturbing images of German or Japanese soldiers. These posters were meant to stir up hatred for enemies. To do so, some posters used racist **stereotypes**.

The OWI produced films and radio shows, too. Short films were shown in theaters before movies. These films told stories with specific messages.

An OWI artist draws a soldier, a sailor, and a welder for a poster celebrating American workers.

Some warned people not to give secrets to the enemy. Others explained the need for rationing and recycling.

Newsreels also played before movies. These short films gave news about the war. Some showed soldiers or battles. But most focused on positive events. By leaving out negative parts of the war, they helped maintain support for it.

In the OWI's radio shows, actors performed stories. Most stories were about military victories. They were meant to boost morale. Some stories were about cruel enemy acts. They were meant to unite Americans against Japan and Germany. Most stories were not real. But they were often based on facts.

Other groups created propaganda as well. For example, factory owners made posters to help increase production. Comic books featured stories with superheroes fighting enemy soldiers. And several comic book characters urged readers to buy war bonds.

Enemy propaganda spread in the United States, too. This propaganda aimed to build support for Japan or Germany. It tried to make Americans

Actors rehearse for an OWI radio show about the dangers of Nazi Germany.

give up on fighting. Some Americans did become discouraged. But in general, support for the war stayed strong.

World War II also shaped entertainment that was not propaganda. Many books, films, and songs focused on soldiers or the home front. This remained true long after the war's end in 1945. World War II and its impacts continue to appear in American media today.

FOCUS ON

THE US HOME FRONT

Write your answers on a separate piece of paper.

1. Write a paragraph describing the goals of the Double Victory campaign.

2. Do you think the United States was right to stay neutral at the start of the war? Why or why not?

3. Which term refers to limiting the amounts of certain goods that people can buy?

    A. production
    B. propaganda
    C. rationing

4. Why was research an important part of the US war effort during World War II?

    A. New technology helped the country predict the war.
    B. New information helped the country stay out of the war.
    C. New weapons helped the country fight and defeat enemies.

Answer key on page 48.

GLOSSARY

allies
Nations or people that are on the same side during a war.

censorship
The act of changing or deleting information in order to prevent it from spreading.

civilians
People who are not in the military.

civil rights
Rights that protect people's freedom and equality.

discrimination
Unfair treatment of a person or group based on race, gender, or other factors.

morale
The mood of a group of people, especially people in a difficult situation.

patriotic
Showing love or support for one's country.

racism
Hatred or mistreatment of people because of their skin color or ethnicity.

radar
An instrument that locates things by bouncing radio waves off them.

stereotypes
Oversimplified, unfair, or untrue ideas about what all members of a certain group are like.

TO LEARN MORE

BOOKS

Gale, Ryan. *The Manhattan Project*. Minneapolis: Abdo Publishing, 2021.

MacCarald, Clara. *Children in Japanese American Confinement Camps*. Lake Elmo, MN: Focus Readers, 2019.

Simons, Lisa M. Bolt. *The U.S. WASP: Trailblazing Women Pilots of World War II*. North Mankato, MN: Capstone Press, 2018.

NOTE TO EDUCATORS

Visit **www.focusreaders.com** to find lesson plans, activities, links, and other resources related to this title.

INDEX

Answer Key: 1. Answers will vary; **2.** Answers will vary; **3.** C; **4.** C